D1129829

Sea Mammals

Sea Mammals

REBECCA STEFOFF

Marshall Cavendish
Benchmark
New York

With thanks to Paul L. Sieswerda, Aquarium Curator, New York Aquarium, for his expert review of the manuscript.

Marshall Cavendish Benchmark
99 White Plains Road
Tarrytown, New York 10591
www.marshallcavendish.us

Editor: Karen Ang
Publisher: Michelle Bisson
Art Director: Anahid Hamparian
Series Designer: Patrice Sheridan

Library of Congress Cataloging-in-Publication Data
Stefoff, Rebecca, date
Sea mammals / by Rebecca Stefoff.
p. cm.
Includes bibliographical references and index.
Summary: "Explores the habitats, life cycles, and other characteristics of
sea mammals"—Provided by publisher.
ISBN 978-0-7614-3072-8
1. Marine mammals--Juvenile literature. I. Title.
QL713.2S74 2009
599.5—dc22
2008011452

Front cover: A Florida manatee
Title page: An orca, or killer whale
Back cover: A whale tail

Photo Research by Candlepants Incorporated
Cover Photo: Pacific Stock/Superstock
The photographs in this book are used by permission and through the courtesy of:
Shutterstock: , 3, 7, 13, 19, 22, 23, 29, 39, 24, 27, 55, 63, 64, 66, 67,
70, 73, 76, 77, 85, back cover. Minden Pictures: Flip Nicklin, 6, 42, 81;
Hiroya Minakuchi, 40, 50; Chris Newbert, 43; Todd Pusser/ Npl, 59; Fred
Bavendam, 60. Corbis: Academy Of Natural Sciences Of Philadelphia, 9;
Historical Picture Archive, 11; Stuart Westmorland, 61. AP Images: The News
Tribune, Dean Koepfler, 18; Petar Petrov, 79; Tasmanian Parks And Wildlife
Service, Liz Wren, HO, 82. Alamy Images: Chad Ehlers, 21; Brandon Cole
Marine Photography, 38, 45; Wildlife Gmbh, 46; David Fleetham, 49, 84;
Stephen Frink Collection, 51; Rhk Uw Productions, 52; Blickwinkel, 56;
Louise Murray, 57; Kevin Schafer, 68; Mark Bowler, 72; Scphotos, 74; Bryan &
Cherry Alexander Photography, 75. Getty Images: Cris Bouroncle/AFP, 28;
William West/AFP, 33; Chris Wilkins/AFP, 80. Photo Researchers Inc.: Richard
Ellis, 31, 35; Christian Darkin/Spl, 32; Mark Carwardine/Nhpa, 78. Super
Stock: Corbis, 54; Age Fotostock, 62.

Printed in Malaysia
1 3 5 6 4 2

CONTENTS

A blue whale glides through the Sea of Cortez, off the coast of Mexico's Baja Peninsula. During the winter, some blue whales gather here to feed and give birth in subtropical waters.

Classifying Life

The biggest animal that has ever lived on Earth is the blue whale. Even the largest dinosaurs were smaller than these immense creatures, which swim majestically through all of the world's oceans today. Blue whales range in length from 66 to 110 feet (20 to 33.5 meters) and weigh between 80 and 150 tons (72.5 and 136 metric tons). They are many times more massive than the largest living land animals, the elephants, which reach a maximum weight of just under 8 tons (7.25 metric tons).

Yet blue whales and elephants have something in common. Both are mammals, warm-blooded creatures that give birth to live young and nurse their offspring with milk from special organs called mammary glands. Blue whales, however, spend their entire lives in water. So do the other eighty or so species of whales, dolphins, and porpoises that are the blue whale's closest relatives. They are sometimes called marine mammals because their habitat, the ocean, is a marine environment.

The ocean is home to other mammals as well. Like cattle of the sea, large, slow-moving manatees and dugongs graze on undersea pastures in the warm waters of the world, never coming onto land. Sea otters dive deep into the kelp forests that rise from the ocean floor, floating on the surface to rest. Seals and sea lions hunt beneath the waves, but from time to time they clamber onto coastal rocks, beaches, and piers. Polar bears spend a large part of their lives hunting on the Arctic ice, and they can swim for long distances through the cold northern oceans.

Sea mammals are closer biologically to land mammals than they are to the fish who share the oceans with them. At the same time, the sea mammals are extremely well suited to life in the water. From enormous whales to small otters and porpoises, they have different histories and habits. To understand how these marine mammals are related to each other, and how they fit into the natural world, it helps to know something about how scientists classify living things.

THE INVENTION OF TAXONOMY

Science gives us tools for making sense of the natural world. One of the most powerful tools is classification, which means organizing things in a pattern according to their differences and similarities. Since ancient times, scientists who study living things have been developing a classification system for living things. This system is called taxonomy. Scientists use taxonomy to group together organisms that share features, setting them apart from other organisms with different features.

Taxonomy is hierarchical, which means that it is arranged in levels. The highest levels are categories that include many kinds of organisms. These large categories are divided into smaller categories, which in turn are divided into still smaller ones. The most basic category is the species, a single kind of organism.

The idea behind taxonomy is simple, but the world of living things is complex and full of surprises. Taxonomy is not a fixed pattern. It keeps changing to reflect new knowledge or ideas. Over time, scientists have developed rules for adjusting the pattern even when they disagree on the details.

One of the first taxonomists was the ancient Greek philosopher Aristotle (384-322 BCE), who investigated many branches of science, including biology. Aristotle arranged living things on a sort of ladder, or scale. At the bottom were those he considered lowest, or least developed, such as worms. Above them were things he considered higher, or more developed, such as fish, then birds, then mammals.

For centuries after Aristotle, taxonomy made little progress. People who studied nature tended to group organisms together by features that were easy to see, such as separating trees from grasses or birds from fish. However, they did not try to develop a system for classifying all life. Then, between 1682 and 1705, an English naturalist named John Ray published a plan of the living world that was designed to have a place for every species of plant and animal. Ray's system was hierarchical, with several levels of larger and smaller categories. It was the foundation of modern taxonomy.

This sixteenth-century image of a seal may look odd to modern eyes, but it was part of an early effort to understand the sea mammals and their place in the scheme of life.

Swedish naturalist Carolus Linnaeus (1707-1778) built on that foundation to create the taxonomic system used today. Linnaeus was chiefly interested in plants, but his system of classification included all living things. Its highest level of classification was the kingdom. To Linnaeus, everything belonged to either the plant kingdom or the animal kingdom. Each of these kingdoms was divided into a number of smaller categories called classes. Each class was divided into orders. Each order was divided into genera. Each genus (the singular form of genera) contained one or more species.

Linnaeus also developed another of Ray's ideas, a method for naming species. Before Linnaeus published his important work *System of Nature* in 1735, scientists had no recognized system for referring to plants and animals. Organisms were generally known by their common names, but many of them had different names in various countries. As a result, two naturalists might call the same plant or animal by two different names—or use the same name for two different organisms. Linnaeus wanted to end such confusion, so that scholars everywhere could communicate clearly about plants and animals. He started the practice of giving each plant or animal a two-part scientific name made up of its genus and species. These names were in Latin, the scientific language of Linnaeus's day. For example, the blue whale's scientific name is *Balaenoptera musculus* (or *B. musculus* after the first time the full name is used). The genus *Balaenoptera* contains five species of whales. The blue whale is set apart from the other four species by the second part of its name, *musculus.*

Linnaeus named hundreds of species. Other scientists quickly adopted his highly flexible system to name many more. The Linnaean system appeared at a time when European naturalists were exploring the rest of the world and finding thousands of new plants and animals. This flood of discoveries was overwhelming at times, but Linnaean taxonomy helped scientists identify and organize their finds.

TAXONOMY TODAY

Biologists still use the system of scientific naming that Linnaeus developed. Anyone who discovers a new species can choose its scientific name, which is usually Latin, or once in a while Greek. Other aspects of taxonomy, though, have changed since Linnaeus's time.

Over the years, as biologists learned more about the similarities and differences among living things, they added new levels to taxonomy. Eventually, an organism's full classification could include the following

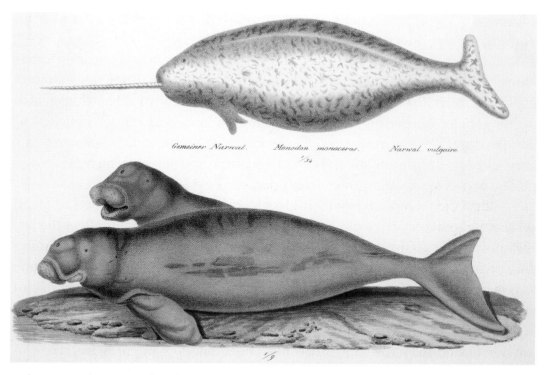

Gemeiner Narwal.   *Monodon monoceros.*   *Narwal vulgaire.*

By the nineteenth century, when these drawings were made, scientists had encountered marine mammals around the world, including the narwhal (top) of the northern polar seas and the dugong (bottom) of tropical waters.

taxonomic levels: kingdom, subkingdom, phylum (some biologists use division instead of phylum for plants and fungi), subphylum, superclass, class, subclass, infraclass, order, superfamily, family, genus, species, and subspecies or variety.

Another change concerned the kinds of information that scientists use to classify organisms. The earliest naturalists used obvious physical features, such as the differences between fish and birds, to divide organisms into groups. By the time of Ray and Linnaeus, naturalists could study specimens in more detail. Aided by new tools such as the microscope, they explored the inner structures of plants and animals. For a long time after Linnaeus, classification was based mainly on details of anatomy, or physical structure, although scientists also looked at how an organism reproduced and how and where it lived.

Today, biologists can peer more deeply into an organism's inner workings than Aristotle or Linnaeus ever dreamed possible. They can look inside its individual cells and study the arrangement of DNA that makes up its genetic blueprint. Genetic information is key to modern classification because DNA is more than an organism's blueprint. DNA also reveals how closely the organism is related to other species and how long ago those species separated during the process of evolution.

In recent years, many biologists have pointed out that the Linnaean system is a patchwork of old and new ideas. It doesn't clearly reflect the latest knowledge about the evolutionary links among organisms both living and extinct. Some scientists now call for a new approach to taxonomy, one that is based entirely on evolutionary relationships. One of the most useful new approaches is called phylogenetics, the study of organisms' evolutionary histories. In this approach, scientists group together all organisms that are descended from the same ancestor. The result is branching, treelike diagrams called cladograms. These cladograms show the order in which groups of plants or animals split off from their shared ancestors.

None of the proposed new systems of classifying living things has been accepted by all scientists, but the move toward a phylogenetic

Manatees are tranquil, slow-moving creatures that graze on plants in warm, shallow water. They are descended from land mammals whose front legs have evolved into flippers.

approach is under way. Still, scientists continue to use the two main features of Linnaean taxonomy: the hierarchy of categories and the two-part species name. Expert may disagree about the proper term for a category, however, or about how to classify a particular plant or animal. Because scientists create and use classifications for many different purposes, there is no single "right" way to classify organisms.

Even at the highest level of classification, scientists take different approaches to taxonomy. A few of them still divide all life into two kingdoms, plants and animals. At the other extreme are scientists who divide life into thirteen or more kingdoms, possibly grouping the kingdoms into larger categories called domains or superkingdoms. Most scientists, though, use classification systems with five to seven kingdoms: plants, animals, fungi, and several kingdoms of microscopic organisms such as bacteria, amoebas, and algae.

How Taxonomy Works: The Florida Manatee

If you swim or snorkel in the clear waters around the Florida coast, you may find yourself face to face with a creature that gazes at you from a pair of brown eyes over a whiskery, potato-shaped muzzle. Its plump, 3-meter-long (9.8-foot-long), gray-brown body drifts slowly through the water, guided by paddlelike flippers on each side. Then, with a lazy flap of its broad, flat tail, the animal sails away across the sandy bottom.

You've met a West Indian manatee, *Trichesis manatus*. These harmless vegetarians live along the east coast of the Americas. They come in two subspecies, or varieties. *T. manatus manatus,* the Antillean manatee, is found from Brazil north to Mexico. *T. manatus latirostris,* the Florida manatee, lives along the U.S. coast from Texas to Virginia, but as its name suggests, it is most common around the Florida peninsula. Manatees gather there to warm themselves in the sunny coastal waters, munch seagrass, and bear their young.

Here is the Florida manatee's scientific classification, from largest category to smallest:

Kingdom	Animalia (animals)
Phylum	Chordata (animals with spinal cords)
Subphylum	Vertebrata (animals with spinal cords and segmented spines)
Superclass	Tetrapoda (animals with four limbs: amphibians, reptiles, birds, and mammals)
Class	Mammalia (mammals, which are tetrapods that have hair, give birth to live young, and nurse their young with milk from mammary glands)
Order	Sirenia (aquatic mammals with paddlelike front limbs, no hind limbs, and flat tails; includes manatees and dugongs; sometimes called sea cows)
Family	Trichechidae (manatees)
Genus	*Trichechus* (three species of manatees)
Species	*manatus* (West Indian manatee; has two varieties or subspecies)
Subspecies	*latirostris* (Florida manatee)

The classification of living things is always changing as scientists learn more about the connections among organisms. Whales, for example, have moved from branch to branch on the taxonomic tree. In 1735 the pioneering taxonomist Linnaeus classified whales as fishes. Whales lived in the sea, and their bodies were shaped a lot like those of sharks and other large fishes. A few decades later, however, Linnaeus changed his mind and created a new taxonomic order for whales, because he had recognized that they were mammals, not related to fishes. In the next century, scientists studied the anatomy, or physical structure, of whales. As they examined skulls and skeletons, they realized that whales share many anatomical features with a group of hoofed mammals that scientists call the artiodactyls—even though, on the outside, a whale doesn't look much like a hippo or a sheep! In recent years, fossil finds and DNA research have shown that whales, hippos, pigs, sheep, deer, and camels all evolved from the same distant ancestor. Based on these insights, some scientists now group whales and artiodactyls together in a new superorder called Cetartiodactyla.

Marine mammals are challenging to study. They spend much of their lives underwater, sometimes in the deep oceans. Some of them are rare and difficult to locate. Others are simply too huge to be studied in captivity. Although humans have hunted and observed sea mammals for thousands of years, we have much to learn about their lives and habits. How do sea mammals interact with each other and with other animals? What do they communicate to each other? How intelligent are they? What can we do to preserve these animals and their environment? These are just some of the questions that draw biologists and wildlife researchers into the watery world of sea mammals.

Scientists classify living things in arrangements like this family tree of the animal
Sea mammals belong to different families

ANIMAL

PHYLA

CNIDARIANS

Coral

ARTHROPODS

(Animals with
external skeletons
and
jointed limbs)

MOLLUSKS

Octopus

SUB PHYLA

CLASSES

CRUSTACEANS

Lobster

ARACHNIDS

Spider

INSECTS

Butterfly

MYRIAPODS

Centipede

ORDERS

CARNIVORES

Walrus

SIRENIANS

Manatee

CETACEANS

Dolphin

PRIMATES

Monkey

kingdom to highlight the connections and the differences among the many forms of life.
within the carnivore, sirenian, and cetacean orders.

KINGDOM

ANNELIDS

Earthworm

CHORDATES

(Animals
with a
dorsal
nerve chord)

ECHINODERMS

Starfish

VERTEBRATES

(Animals
with a
backbone)

FISH

Fish

BIRDS

Penguin

MAMMALS

AMPHIBIANS

Frog

REPTILES

Snake

HERBIVORES
(5 ORDERS)

Horse

RODENTS

Squirrel

INSECTIVORES

Hedgehog

MARSUPIALS

Kangaroo

SMALL MAMMALS
(SEVERAL ORDERS)

Rabbit

Killer whales break the surface near Washington State's San Juan Islands. The spray above them, called blow, jets upward when whales breathe out forcefully through their blowholes. Blow consists of vapor that forms when warm air from the whales' lungs meets cooler air, although it may also contain natural fluids from the lungs. One of the easiest ways to spot whales at sea is to look for blow.

Marine Mammals of the World

Sea mammals are not a single branch on the tree of life. They come from different branches that adapted to marine life independently. For this reason, "sea mammals" is not a taxonomic category. It's simply a useful label that includes the many kinds of mammals that live in the oceans.

Around 120 or 130 species of sea mammals exist today. The number varies from list to list because some scientists are "lumpers" and some are "splitters." When two animals are very similar, a lumper tends to think that they belong to the same species. A splitter, on the other hand, focuses on the differences between the two and may be more likely to see them as separate species. For example, lumpers think that the sea lion of Japan belongs to the same species as the sea lion of California. They call the Japanese sea lion *Zalophus californianus japonicus*, a name that identifies it as a subspecies, or regional variety, of the California sea lion. Splitters, however, call the Japanese sea lion *Zalophus japonicus*, a name that identifies it as a distinct species. The classification of the Japanese sea lion no longer matters as much as it once did, however. These marine mammals have not been seen since the 1950s, and many authorities consider them extinct.

Even if scientists don't always agree about species, the big picture of sea mammal taxonomy is clear. All sea mammals belong to three orders within the mammal class. One is the order Cetacea, which is made up of whales, dolphins, and porpoises. Another is the order Sirenia, which is made up of dugongs and manatees. The third order is Carnivora, which is made up of many families of carnivores, or flesh-eating mammals. The sea mammals from this order are the seals, sea lions, walruses, sea otters, and polar bears.

Anyone who watches nature shows on television or reads nature books is familiar with some sea mammals. Dolphins, sea otters, dramatic black-and-white killer whales, and majestic blue whales are among the varieties that scientists have studied in detail. Many books have been written about these animals, but other sea mammals are less well known. Even marine biologists have little solid information about the beaked whales, for example. These cetaceans live in remote parts of the ocean, spend little time at the surface, and have never been commercially hunted as other whale species have been. Still, sea mammals as a group are much better studied than many other kinds of animals, with plenty of information available about particular families and species. One useful way to look at sea mammals is to focus on some of the ways they are alike and different.

THE MAMMAL HERITAGE

The lives of sea mammals are shaped in part by the fact that they *are* mammals. In terms of their life cycles and social behavior, sea mammals are much like land animals. Where mating is concerned, for example, most sea mammals follow a very common mammalian pattern. Called polygyny, this pattern of reproduction means that individual males mate with multiple females during each mating season.

Polygyny can take many forms. For example, male and female sea otters spend a brief time together and then separate, and the male seeks

Beluga whales have been called "sea canaries" because, like the small birds known as canaries, they make a wide variety of chirping, squeaking, and singing sounds.

other partners. Polar bear mating habits are similar, with male bears moving around from one female to another. Other sea mammals carry out their mating rituals in a group setting. Many species of fur seal and sea lions gather in great numbers each year on the beaches and islands that are their traditional breeding grounds. There the males compete to attract, defend, and mate with as many females as possible.

Among the northern fur seals and some other species, males reach the breeding grounds first. Adult males claim individual breeding sites—places where females can comfortably raise their young—and defend these territories from other males. This is often done simply with bluster and shoving, but sometimes with real fighting. The bigger and better-defended territories attract the most females, and the defender mates with them all.

Males of other species, such as elephant seals, take a different approach. Instead of defending the territory, they defend the females. They gather females into bands called harems and prevent other males from mating with them. Researchers who have studied elephant seals report that more than 90 percent of all males never get the chance to mate in their lifetimes. However, strong, aggressive males who successfully defend their harems may mate with more than a hundred females, passing their genetic heritage on to many descendants.

Another requirement of mammalian life is parental care. Mammals give birth to live offspring that need to be fed and cared for after they are born. In all sea mammal species, mothers tend their young on their own, with no parenting help from the fathers. For female whales and sirenians,

A stretch of beach becomes a crowded seal colony at breeding time.

Gray seals live along coastlines and around islands on both sides of the North Atlantic Ocean. In the United States, people often spot gray seals off the New England coast.

who give birth in the water, the responsibility begins immediately. Newborns must quickly take their first breath of air, or they will die, so mothers often nudge or push their young to the surface. Afterward, sea mammal mothers nurse their offspring. The offspring are called calves if they are whales or sirenians, pups if they are seals or sea otters, and cubs if they are polar bears.

Most sea mammal mothers give birth to a single offspring at a time. Whales occasionally have twins, and polar bears can have as many as three cubs in a litter. Depending upon the species, young sea mammals may remain with their mothers for several years, although most become fairly independent within a year.

23

Social Lives

Sea mammals, like land mammals, have a wide range of social organizations. Scientists do not know whether every species of sea mammal is solitary or sociable. When breeding season is over and whales and seals are spread across the ocean, far from land, the lives of animals in some species are something of a mystery. Researchers do know, however, that many whales and dolphins associate more or less permanently in groups called

A sea lion at a marine research laboratory is learning to place a scientific device onto a model of a whale. When used on a real whale, the device will record the time and depth of the whale's dives. People have trained sea lions and other marine mammals to perform many undersea tasks, both scientific and military.

pods, with close bonds among individuals. In contrast, polar bears are almost entirely solitary. Manatees fall somewhere in between. They often travel in loose-knit groups of four to eight animals, although some are solitary and others form large but temporary herds. Sea otters are similar—they spend a lot of time alone but seem to enjoy being around other otters. As many as a hundred sea otters may "raft" together, resting on their backs on the surface of the sea.

Dolphins—one family of whales—are famous for their intelligence. Entertainments such as the movie *Free Willy*, which told of the connection between a boy and a killer whale, and the old TV show *Flipper*, about the adventures of a clever dolphin, fed the image of these mammals as highly intelligent, but science has contributed, too. Although intelligence is very hard to measure (even in humans), researchers have found that dolphins and their relatives, including killer whales, learn new things extremely fast. Dolphins and some species of whales can communicate over long distances by making distinctive sounds, although it is impossible to know for sure what they are saying.

Sea lions are also clever and fairly easy to train. Most circus "seals," in fact, are sea lions, which are better than seals at learning tricks. The U.S. Navy has trained both dolphins and sea lions to perform military tasks such as clearing explosive mines from the sea.

LIFE IN A MARINE ENVIRONMENT

The mammal heritage has shaped sea mammals, but so has the sea. Adaptations for aquatic life have created major differences between marine mammals and their cousins on land. Take legs—they're very useful on land, but not so useful underwater. In most species of sea mammals, forelimbs have evolved into flippers, and hind limbs have either become flippers or disappeared. Hair has changed, too. All mammals have some hair at some point in their lives, even if it is before they are born. Some sea

MARINE MAMMAL SKELETONS

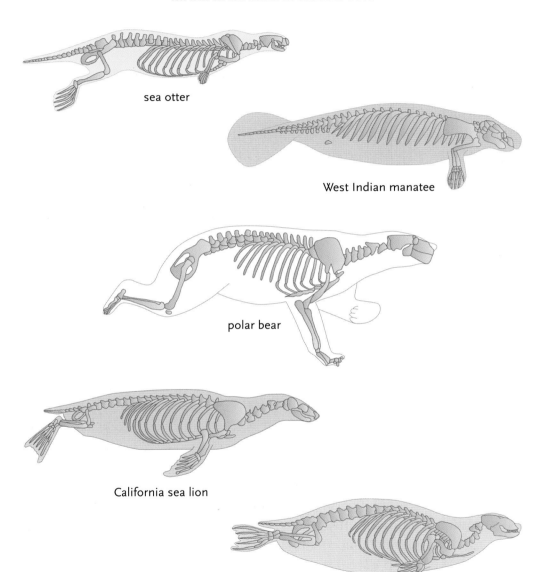

sea otter

West Indian manatee

polar bear

California sea lion

harbor seal

A seal pup explores its watery world. Over millions of years, mammals that once lived on land have become magnificently adapted to life in the oceans of the world.

mammals, however, have lost their hair, or almost lost it—whiskers and a few scattered hairs are all that remain on whales and sirenians.

Many marine mammals are quite large. When an ocean-dwelling species evolves toward a bigger size, it gains several advantages. First, it takes less energy and effort to support a large body in the ocean than on land, because the pressure of the water helps to support the body. A blue whale could never live on land, even if it had legs—its massive body would require a skeleton so big that it would collapse under its own weight. Second, larger animals have less surface area (skin), compared to their overall volume (body mass), than smaller animals. A big sea-dwelling creature finds it easier to conserve warmth inside its body, while a small creature loses more heat into the water through its skin.

Breathing air when they live in water, adjusting to the salt that is everywhere in the marine environment, learning to see and hear underwater with the help of new sense organs—mammals have made these and other adaptations to life in the sea. The long shift from land to water continues today as sea mammals continue the journey that began millions of years ago, when the first mammals stepped from the land into the sea.

The fossilized skeleton of a whale that lived 40 million years ago sprawls across the Egyptian desert where the waves of an ancient sea once rolled. Wind and the careful work of scientists have exposed hundreds of fossils in a region of Egypt called Wadi el-Hutan.

Back to the Ocean

Life on Earth started in the sea several billion years ago. Millions of years later, some kinds of life migrated to the land. Later still, one group of land-dwelling animals developed into mammals. Then a reverse migration took place—some mammals returned to the ocean.

The oceans had advantages. They offered habitat and food sources that mammals could use. To do so, however, they evolved some features that made them better adapted to life in the oceans. Some marine mammals started that process of evolution long ago. They have had so much time to adapt that they are now very different from their closest relatives on land. Others began their journey back to the sea much more recently, and they are not so different from land mammals.

The first mammals to become sea mammals were the whales. By about 52 million years ago, their ancestors had started to spend part of their lives in water. Since that time, whales have evolved so far away from their ancestral forms that they cannot leave the oceans—although, like all sea mammals, they need air and must come to the surface to breathe.

While the whales were evolving and adapting to marine life, other kinds of mammals also went back to the sea. The latest were the polar bears. Although they are considered marine mammals, they still spend a significant part of their lives on solid ground, or at least on solid ice.

AMONG THE ANCIENT MAMMALS

Before there were mammals, there were reptiles. For millions of years reptiles were the dominant form of animal life in the sea and on land. They evolved into a great variety of forms. Scientists call one group of them mammal-like reptiles because they appear to have started developing the physical features of mammals, such as hair, warm-bloodedness, and glands that produced milk to feed the young.

The first true mammals, descended from some of the mammal-like reptiles, appeared between 225 and 200 million years ago. Fossils of these early mammals show that they were small animals. Scientists think that they resembled today's shrews, which roam fields and forest floors, eating insects, worms, and birds' eggs.

By 120 million years ago, mammals were evolving in several directions. One group, called creodonts, contained the ancestors of all modern carnivores—meat-eaters such as weasels, bears, dogs, and cats. Another group, called condylarths, included the ancestors of all modern ungulates, or animals with hoofs—cows, horses, deer, hippos, giraffes, antelope, and more.

Marine mammals are among the descendants of the condylarths and the creodonts. Two modern orders of sea mammals evolved from branches of the ancient condylarth group. These are the cetaceans (whales, dolphins, and porpoises) and the sirenians or sea cows (dugongs and manatees). The rest of the modern sea mammals—seals, sea lions, walruses, sea otters, and polar bears—evolved from the creodont line.

FIRST WHALES

The oldest known fossils of marine mammals are bones of whales that lived 52 million years ago. Scientists call these early whales archaeocetes, which is Latin for "old whales."

The first archaeocetes did not look much like modern whales. For one thing, they had legs. Scientists have named one genus of archaeocetes *Ambulocetus*, which means "walking whale." It had short but sturdy legs, toes that ended in hoofs, and a pointed tail. Paleontologists, scientists who study ancient and extinct life forms, think that these creatures lived a lot like modern hippopotamuses, partly on land and partly in fresh water.

As whales evolved into a range of forms, they spent more time in the water. Eventually they began to lose their legs. A species called *Rodhocetus* looked something like a modern crocodile, with long, toothed jaws. Like crocodiles, it may have preyed on fish and other fast-moving water creatures. The basilosaurines were a group of ancient whales that flourished around 40 million years ago. Some of them were close to 82 feet (25 meters) long. *Basilosaurus isis* is the best-known member of this

Ambulocetus, the "walking whale," was an early ancestor of the whales. It probably divided its time between land and water.

31

The ancient whale *Basilosaurus,* shown here in a computer-generated image, had long jaws and sharp teeth. Marks on its fossil teeth show that *Basilosaurus,* like many modern whales, ate fish and squid.

group because paleontologists have found hundreds of its skeletons in Egypt. *B. isis* had short forelimbs, but its tiny, almost invisible hind limbs were useless for either walking or swimming. It was well on the way to leglessness.

Modern whales probably descended from a group of small archaeocetes called dorudontines. These ancient whales looked something like dolphins and were fully adapted to aquatic life, with front limbs that had become flippers. Many evolutionary changes took place in the millions of years between the dorudontines and the modern whales, dolphins, and porpoises. One major change involved the bones of the skull. In a process that scientist call telescoping, the nostrils moved from the front of the skull up to the top of the head and became blowholes. This let cetaceans breathe in and out through the blowholes without lifting their entire heads out of the water.

In 1990, a teenage surfer named Staumn Hunder spotted bones sticking out of a boulder on a beach at Jan Juc, Australia. By 2006 researchers had identified the fossil in the rock as the skull of a 25-million-year-old whale. Called *Janjucetus hunderi* in honor of its finder, it combines features of two different kinds of modern whales: toothed whales and baleen, or toothless, whales.

Another important change happened around 35 million years ago, when whales began evolving into two groups: the odontocetes (toothed whales) and the mysticetes (baleen whales). This ancient division is why scientists today divide the order Cetacea into two suborders, one for each type of whale.

FIRST SIRENIANS

After the whales, the next mammals to adapt to life in the sea were the sirenians, or sea cows. Their ancestors belonged to a group of condylarths called tethytheres. (The name refers to the Tethys Sea, which existed millions of years ago, when the continents were in different positions on the Earth's surface.) One branch of tethytheres eventually gave rise to the proboscids, land-dwelling animals with trunks, such as mammoths and elephants. Another branch evolved into torpedo-shaped aquatic creatures with front flippers and broad tails: the sirenians. Because other creatures related to sirenians became extinct over the years, elephants are the sirenians' closest living relatives.

The oldest known sirenians lived about 50 million years ago. Early varieties such as *Pezosiren, Protosiren,* and *Prorastomus* had legs, unlike modern sirenians. Some species also had tusks—pairs of long curved teeth that stuck out of their mouths, like the tusks of modern elephants or walruses. Paleontologists think that the ancestral sea cows divided their time between land and water. They were herbivores, feeding on grasses and other plants. Fossil teeth show that they ate a lot of sand along with their food, which makes scientists think that they grazed near beaches.

Over tens of millions of years, many sirenian species evolved and then became extinct. Sirenians reached their greatest diversity during the Miocene epoch, which began about 23 million years ago and lasted until 5 million years ago. Another order of sea mammals, the desmostylians, also lived during that time. Desmostylians were four-legged animals about the size and shape of hippos, with short tusks. Related to proboscids and sirenians, the desmostylians lived in freshwater lakes and rivers as well as in shallow seas, but all of the desmostylians died out long ago.

MORE MAMMALS TAKE TO THE SEA

Whales and sirenians descended from the ancient mammals called condylarths, which also gave rise to the hoofed, plant-eating mammals. All of the other sea mammals descended from the carnivorous, or flesh-eating, creodonts. They evolved from a group of creodont descendants called arctoids. Raccoons, weasels, and bears also evolved from the arctoid line.

The first carnivorous sea mammals were the pinnipeds, the seals, sea lions, and walruses. Scientists are not yet certain whether pinnipeds are more closely related to the mustelids (weasels, skunks, and their relatives) or to the ursids (bears). They are fairly sure, however, that pinnipeds originated in the northern Pacific region. The earliest known pinniped fossils are about 27 million years old and come from Oregon. Other early remains have been found in Japan and California. As pinnipeds developed into a variety of forms, they spread into other waters of the world. By about 11 million years ago the pinnipeds had divided into three families that still exist today: the earless seals; the eared seals and sea lions; and the walruses.

Meanwhile, other members of the arctoid line were experimenting with aquatic life. One group of mustelids became otters. They kept the basic weasel body plan—a long, narrow, flexible body with short, powerful legs—but evolved into superb swimmers. Most otter species lived in rivers and lakes, but some also hunted in bays or river mouths where fresh water mingled with salt water. A few adapted to full-time life in the sea. The earliest fossils of modern sea otters date from about 1 to 3 million years ago.

The world's newest marine mammal is the polar bear, *Ursus maritimus.* The oldest known polar bear fossils are only about 100,000 years old, but scientists who have studied bear DNA think that polar bears evolved in the Arctic from brown bears (also known as grizzlies) much earlier—perhaps 1 million years ago. Although all eight living species of bears can swim, and some of them regularly venture into rivers to catch fish, the polar bear is the only one that is considered a marine mammal. It depends on the ocean for survival, like all of the world's sea mammals.

Paleoparadoxia and its relatives grazed on offshore plants along the North Pacific coasts. This family of marine mammals flourished for about 10 million years, then became extinct 10 million years ago, leaving no descendants in the modern world.

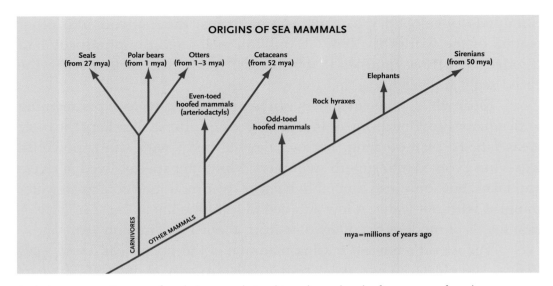

ORIGINS OF SEA MAMMALS

Seals
(from 27 mya)

Polar bears
(from 1 mya)

Otters
(from 1–3 mya)

Cetaceans
(from 52 mya)

Sirenians
(from 50 mya)

Elephants

Even-toed
hoofed mammals
(arteriodactyls)

Rock hyraxes

Odd-toed
hoofed mammals

CARNIVORES

OTHER MAMMALS

mya=millions of years ago

A cladogram, or diagram of evolutionary relationships, shows that the five groups of modern sea mammals descended from different land-dwelling ancestors. Sea mammals share many physical features because all of them have adapted to ocean life.

CONVERGENT EVOLUTION

If sea mammals evolved independently, why are they so much alike in certain ways, even beyond the basic features that all mammals share? Why do cetaceans, sirenians, and pinnipeds all have flippers? Why do whales, walruses, and polar bears all have thick layers of fat beneath their skins?

The answer lies in a process that scientists call convergent evolution. Organisms that evolve along separate lines of inheritance can end up with similar features if they share similar habits or environments. Bats and barn swallows are both agile flyers that prey on flying insects, for example, but bats are mammals and barn swallows are birds. Neither of them is descended from or directly related to the other, but both of them are adapted to a similar way of life.

Convergent evolution explains why sea mammals that evolved separately share so many features. Although they followed different paths, all of

Beach Bears and Swimming Sloths

The great majority of sea mammal species that have ever lived are now extinct. Most of them disappeared millions of years ago. Sometimes, though, fossil finds bring these lost species to light. From skulls found on beaches in Washington State and Oregon, we know that a large marine mammal with big teeth and powerful jaws lived in that region around 10 million years ago. Scientists call it *Kolponomos*. They used to think that it was related to raccoons, but recent research shows that it was more closely related to bears and extinct otters. *Kolponomos* probably lived and fed along beaches, using its fangs to pry clams and mussels off the rocks and then crushing the shells with its massive jaws to get at the meat inside.

In the late 1970s paleontologists digging on the coast of Peru in South America found some surprising fossils: the remains of a marine sloth. The scientists were surprised because all living sloths are arboreal, adapted to life in trees. Some extinct species are called ground sloths because they lived on the ground, but no one ever expected to find evidence of a sea sloth. Paleontologist Greg McDonald later said, "We've been joking that our next trip will be to find the flying sloth." Since that first find, researchers have learned that at least five species of *Thalassocnus*, or marine sloth, lived along Peru's Pacific coast from about 10 to 3 million years ago. These swimming sloths probably used strong hind legs and flexible tails to push themselves through the water as they ate sea grass and other aquatic plants.

them ended up in the same place: the ocean. They did not all adapt to marine life in exactly the same ways, but often they adapted in similar ways to the challenges of breathing, eating, raising their young, and living in the sea.

A humpback whale breaches, hurling its body up out of the water. On rare occasions a whale's entire body leaves the water. More often, especially with large whales, between 40 and 90 percent of the body clears the surface. Scientists think that whales may breach to communicate with other whales or to stun fish when they hit the water.

Cetaceans: Whales, Dolphins, and Porpoises

"There's one! To starboard!" As soon as the cry goes up, everyone on the whale-watching cruise rushes to the starboard (seafaring language for "right") side of the boat, eagerly scanning the ocean's surface. They're looking for a spout of spray, a big curved back breaking above the waves, or possibly the flip of a fluke, as the broad, flat tail of a whale is called. If they're lucky, they'll see the grandest sight a whale-watcher could hope for—a breach. When a whale breaches, its huge body leaps up out of the sea. Dripping water, the whale seems to hang in the air for an instant before crashing back with a shower of spray.

Whale-watching is now a popular activity in many parts of the world. People find whales fascinating for their sheer size and complex social behavior. To many, whales are the ultimate symbols of the oceans and the life they hold.

Whales belong to the order Cetacea, the largest group of sea mammals, with about eighty species. Even though they do not belong to the order Carnivora, cetaceans are meat-eaters. Depending on the species, they feed on prey that can be microscopically small or as big as the giant squid. The cetaceans are divided into two suborders, Odontoceti (toothed whales) and Mysticeti (baleen whales).

TOOTHED WHALES

The suborder of toothed whales contains ten families. Among them are the dolphins and porpoises—which, to taxonomists, are simply small whales. All of the whales in this suborder have teeth, although some species have as few as two of them.

Sperm Whales

Most experts believe that the family Physeteridae has just one species, the sperm whale. This cetacean is found in all the world's oceans. Sperm whales favor regions where the water is at least 3,300 feet (1,000 m) deep, because they are most likely to find squid, their favorite food, in cool, deep parts of the ocean. Only male sperm whales, however, venture into the truly cold waters near the Arctic and Antarctic oceans.

A sperm whale approaches the surface of the ocean to breathe.

Male sperm whales can reach lengths of 59 feet (18 m). Sperm whales are the biggest toothed whales, which means that they are the biggest toothed mammals in the world. (They are also the only whales whose throats are wide enough to swallow a human being whole.)

Inside a sperm whale's large, square-shaped head is an organ filled with a waxy liquid called spermaceti oil. The spermaceti organ is related to the whale's blowhole, or nostrils, and also to sacs inside the body that hold air. Scientists do not know exactly what purpose the spermaceti organ serves, but they suspect that the organ helps the whale use sounds for both communication and navigation.

Sperm whales find their way around underwater by making sounds that bounce or "ping" off objects in the environment. When the whale hears the echoes of the pings, its brain interprets the sounds into a sonic "picture" of the surroundings. This is called echolocation. (Other animals, such as bats, also use echolocation.) Sperm whales may also send out bursts of sound to stun their prey. Many researchers think that the spermaceti organ helps the whales control the sounds they make by acting as a large, fatty "lens" to focus the sound waves. Other kinds of toothed whales use echolocation, too. But they do not have spermaceti organs. Instead, they have pockets of fat called melons on their foreheads that focus the sounds they make.

Two species of cetaceans, the pygmy sperm whale and the dwarf sperm whale, are closely related to the sperm whale. These two whales even have small spermaceti organs. Most scientists, however, place these two species in their own family, the Kogiidae. Adult male dwarf sperm whales measure close to 9 feet (2.7 m) in length. Pygmy sperm whales are slightly larger.

Belugas and Narwhals

The Monodontidae are another family with just two species, the beluga and the narwhal. These cold-loving whales live in and near the Arctic Ocean. Narwhals remain in the northerly waters, while belugas also live in

Wielding their long tusks like a pair of *Star Wars*-style light sabers, two male narwhals spar, probably over a female. Many narwhals bear the scars of such combats.

bays and waterways south of the Arctic, such as the Bering Sea, the Gulf of Alaska, and rivers in Canada and Russia. Occasionally belugas have been seen as far south as Japan and New Jersey. Both the beluga and the narwhal feed on fish, squid, and crustaceans near the sea bottom.

Belugas and narwhals are easy to identify because each species has a distinctive feature. Belugas are the only white whales. Born black, dark gray, or blue-gray, they lighten to a pale cream color, sometimes with brownish spots, by about five years old. The narwhal's special feature is a long pointed tusk that looks like a single horn, found on all males and occasionally on females as well. Some early European explorers tried to pass narwhal tusks off as the horns of mythical unicorns, but the tusk is simply a tooth that grows out from the whale's upper jaw. Tusks are usually a third to half as long as the narwhal's body and may reach lengths of almost 10 feet (3 m).

People have offered many theories about the purpose of the narwhal's tusk. Does the whale use its tusk to poke holes in the ice, to spear prey, or to stir up the bottom for food? Is the tusk somehow involved in echolocation? Today most experts believe tusks are used in fights among narwhals, usually when males compete to mate with females. Many narwhals bear the scars of these conflicts, and whales have been seen "sword-fighting" and even killing each other with their tusks.

Beaked Whales

The family Ziphiidae, the beaked whales, contains about twenty species. They are diverse in size, ranging from 10.8 to 42 feet (3.3 to 12.8 m) in length and weighing between 2,200 and 24,250 pounds (1,000 and 11,000 kilograms). The name "beaked whales" comes from their flat, narrow snouts. Beaked whales have tusklike teeth that stick out from their jaws.

Blainville's beaked whale, also called the dense beaked whale, is a member of the little-known family of beaked whales. This specimen was photographed off the coast of Hawaii's Big Island.

Scientists do not yet know how the whales use these teeth. These cetaceans also have small fins on their backs, usually near their tails Beaked whales may be the least-known cetaceans. They live in all the world's oceans, but never near the coasts. They dive deeply and spend little time at the surface.

Orcas, Pilot Whales, Melon-Headed Whales, and Dolphins

Delphinidae is the largest cetacean family, with more than thirty species. These agile, fast-moving cetaceans are the dolphins, pilot whales, melon-headed whales, and orcas or killer whales. Scientists use the term "delphinids" to refer to the entire family.

The delphinids are widespread—every ocean, sea, and bay has them. Some members of the family are known to swim inland, following large rivers up from the sea. One of these is the smallest delphinid, *Sotalia fluviatilis,* called tucuxi in South America. Some tucuxi are freshwater dolphins that live in the rivers of the Amazon basin. Others are marine dolphins, found in the shallow offshore waters and river mouths of the tropical Atlantic coast. Small tucuxi are about 4.6 feet (1.4 m) long.

The largest delphinid is *Orcinus orca*, the killer whale, which reaches lengths of 32 feet (9.8 m). The name "killer whale" is a little misleading. Orcas are indeed killers—they are highly successful carnivores that sometimes hunt in packs, like wolves, and can bring down such large prey as humpback whales. In fact, orcas are the largest predators that prey on mammals. Wildlife documentaries often show these sleek black-and-white carnivores snatching and devouring seals, although orcas also eat fish, squids, birds, and other non-mammals. Yet orcas are no more murderous than any other predator, and they are not known to be a particular danger to humans. Orca attacks on people are far more rare than attacks by sharks, bears, or other large predators.

The orca is just one of several whales that scientists place in the dolphin family. The others are the pygmy killer whale, the false killer whale, the melon-headed whale, and several species of pilot whales (also called blackfish).

Pacific white-sided dolphins are among the most acrobatic cetaceans. In the wild they often swim alongside boats and ships. In captivity they are popular performers at marine parks.

Dolphins may be the best-known and most-studied cetaceans. They are small—at least compared to sperm whales and blue whales—and very active. Most species regularly breach, jumping completely out of the water. Pods of dolphins often accompany boats and ships, although it is not clear why. Some people think that the animals have learned that food or garbage are often thrown overboard. Others think that dolphins simply enjoy leaping through the waves that boats create. Dolphins are the most acrobatic cetaceans. Captive individuals can easily learn to perform tricks, making them popular entertainments at marine parks. These animals frequently belong to the common bottlenose and Pacific white-sided species.

All but a handful of dolphin species have distinct, flattened snouts like beaked whales. Some species, such as the many kinds of spinner dolphins, have long, fairly pointed beaks. The beaks of other species, such as the white-sided and dusky dolphins, are short and stubby.

Porpoises

Porpoises used to be considered a subgroup of the delphinids, but now the six species of porpoises they are classified in a family of their own, the

Phocoenidae. Like dolphins, porpoises are small cetaceans, but they are less acrobatic and rarely frolic near boats. There are physical differences between dolphins and porpoises as well. Porpoises have blunt, rounded faces without beaks or snouts. And while all dolphins have pointed, cone-shaped teeth, porpoises have teeth with rounded tops, shaped like small spades.

Most porpoises are found along coastlines or near islands, but Dall's porpoise ranges across the North Pacific Ocean. It is the largest porpoise, with a maximum length of 7.9 feet (2.4 m), and has black-and-white coloration like an orca. Another species, the finless porpoise, has adapted to freshwater, life in China's Yangtze River, although most members of the species live in the coastal seas of southern and eastern Asia.

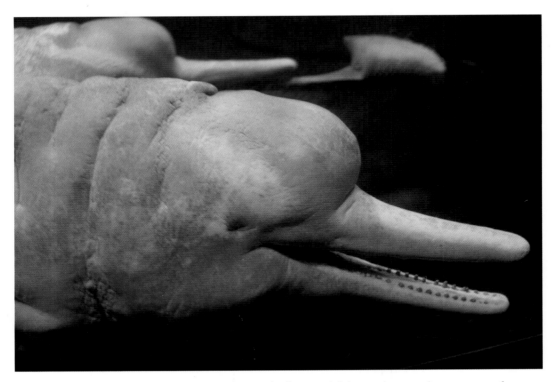

The boto, or Amazon River dolphin, is the largest freshwater dolphin. A boto's color can range from gray to pink to a combination of both.

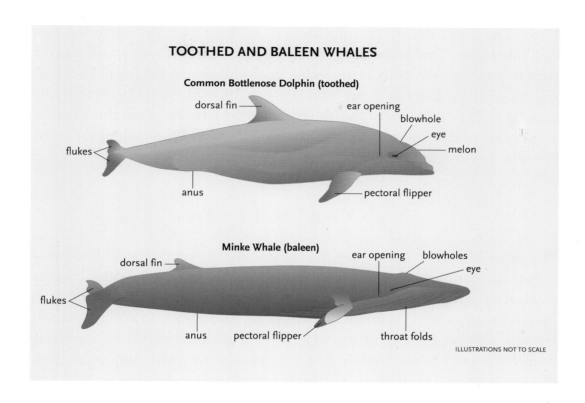

TOOTHED AND BALEEN WHALES

Common Bottlenose Dolphin (toothed)

dorsal fin

ear opening

blowhole

eye

melon

flukes

anus

pectoral flipper

Minke Whale (baleen)

dorsal fin

ear opening

blowholes

eye

flukes

anus

pectoral flipper

throat folds

ILLUSTRATIONS NOT TO SCALE

River Dolphins

The remaining four families of odontocetes, or toothed whales, have just one species in each family. They are the river dolphins. Some of them live in both freshwater rivers and coastal seas. Others are found only in inland river systems. Strictly speaking, these dolphins are not sea mammals, but they closely related to—and descended from—marine dolphins. Like marine dolphins, they feed mainly on fish.

Two river dolphins are South American. The boto or Amazon River dolphin, which varies in color from blue-gray to white to pink, inhabits river systems throughout the northern part of South America. The franciscana or La Plata dolphin is found along the continent's Atlantic coast and in the mouth of the La Plata river between Argentina and Uruguay.

The other two river dolphins live in Asia. *Platanista gangetica* has two subspecies. One is the Ganges River dolphin in northeastern India and Bangladesh, and the other is the Indus River dolphin in Pakistan. The final species of river dolphin is the baiji. This small white cetacean was traditionally called "goddess of the Yangtze" by the Chinese. Like the Yangtze subspecies of the finless porpoise, the baiji lived in China's longest river, but it is now considered extinct.

BALEEN WHALES

The order Mysteceti consists of the baleen whales, sometimes called mysticetes or toothless whales. Some mysticetes are enormous—the biggest creatures on the planet—but the food they eat is so tiny that some of it cannot be seen clearly without a microscope. Mysticetes do not have teeth. Instead, sheets or plates of a tough, flexible material called baleen hang from the roofs of their mouth. The whales feed by swimming with their mouths open and then using their large tongues to force the water back out through the baleen, which traps food items such as zooplankton, the tiny animals that drift through the ocean in immense numbers. There are a dozen or so species of baleen whales in four families.

Gray Whales

The gray whale is the only species in its family. It is medium-sized, measuring about 49 feet (15 m) in length, and usually dark gray in color, blotched with pale markings. Gray whales used to live in both the North Atlantic and the North Pacific, but whale hunters exterminated the Atlantic population by the early eighteenth century. Now most gray whales live along the Pacific coast of North America, migrating each year between Alaska and California or Mexico. A much smaller population of gray whales, perhaps 100 animals or fewer, lives in the western Pacific near Siberia, Japan, and China.

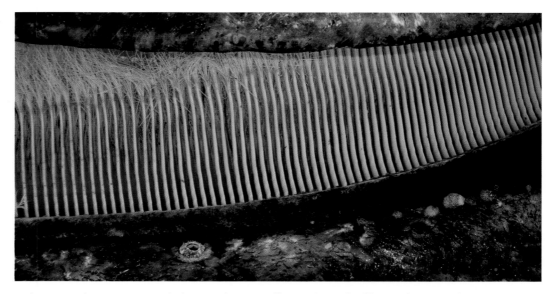

Baleen, seen here in a gray whale's mouth, is an efficient device for filtering food out of seawater. The gray objects on the whale's skin are small, hard-shelled animals called barnacles, a common parasite on cetaceans.

Pygmy Right Whales

The pygmy right whale, *Caperea marginata,* is also the only species in its family. It is the smallest baleen whale, reaching lengths of about 21 feet (6.5 m). This species has been sighted only around South Africa, southern South America, Australia, and New Zealand. As yet, scientists know little about it.

Bowhead and Right Whales

The Balaenidae family contains the bowhead whale (sometimes called the Greenland right whale) and the North Atlantic, North Pacific, and southern species of right whales. The largest member of this family is the bowhead, with a maximum length of around 70 feet (19.8 m) and a maximum weight of 110 tons (100,000 kg), although most individuals are smaller.

The right whales got their name during the early days of the whaling industry. Large vessels went to sea, sometimes for years at a stretch, to

Tourists encounter a gray whale off the Baja coast. Such meetings can fill people with admiration and a desire to "save the whales," but some experts worry that too much up-close tourism may harm whales, perhaps by interfering with breeding or raising young.

hunt baleen whales for the oil from their fat and for their baleen. The oil was used as lamp fuel, while the baleen was used in springs, umbrella rods, whips, and structural supports for women's undergarments. Whalers called these species the "right" whales to hunt because they were slower than other baleen whales and less likely to sink after being killed. Right whales also contained more oil and more baleen than the other mysticetes.

What was right for the whalers, sadly, was all wrong for the whales, who were hunted in vast numbers. In some parts of their former range they became extremely rare, or disappeared. Today researchers estimate that about 8,000 right whales and 10,000 bowheads survive, although populations are dangerously small in some regions. Perhaps only 100 right whales, for example, remain in the North Pacific.

The North Pacific right whale shows that taxonomy is important in political and environmental decision-making. The North Pacific and southern right whales used to be considered subspecies of the North Atlantic right whale, and some authorities still classify them that way. In recent years, however, studies of right whale DNA have shown enough differences among the three groups of right whales that many experts now regard them as three separate species. The International Whaling Commission (IWC), which regulates whale hunting for many nations, has recognized the North Pacific right whale as a species under the name *Eubalena japonica.* So has the U.S. government's National Marine Mammal

The southern right whale belongs to a cetacean family that was driven almost to extinction by the whaling industry. The whales were hunted for oil and baleen.

Sunlight passing through the water near Australia's Great Barrier Reef illuminates a minke whale, the smallest of the rorqual family.

Laboratory (NMML). Recognition as a species has increased the level of legal protection for right whales in the North Pacific, because these whales are now considered an endangered species with a very small population.

Rorquals

The rest of the baleen whales belong to the family Balaenopteridae. These whales are often called rorquals, a Norwegian term that means "furrowed whale." The name refers to the furrows, or folds, that run lengthwise along the throats and chests of whales in this family. Like pleats, the furrows can expand to enlarge the width of the rorqual's mouth. This lets the whale take in more zooplankton, copepods (tiny crustaceans), or small fish. That's a good thing, because the larger baleen whales eat a lot—up to 4,000 pounds (1,800 kg) of food organisms a day. Most rorquals and other baleen whales have feeding seasons, usually in the summer, when their prey is abundant and they can cruise through the water scooping up huge mouth-fuls. At other times of the year they may go for long months with little or no food.

The rorquals vary considerably in size. The largest is the blue whale, the biggest animal that has ever lived. The smallest is the minke, which averages 29.5 feet (9 m) in length—less than a third as long as the biggest blue whales. Rorquals have a more streamlined shape than other baleen whales. Their heads are long and narrow, their bodies are torpedo-shaped, and their fins are tapered. This family includes the blue, humpback, minke, sei, Bryde's, and fin whales. Some authorities recognize a few additional species. In addition, researchers have learned through DNA studies that some whales are hybrids of blue and fin whales, although no one knows how common these hybrid whales are. Could interbreeding between two species of whales be the first step toward the creation of a new species? As with many other questions about cetaceans, the world's most numerous sea mammals, only further research will tell.

Some scholars of mythology have suggested that legends about mermaids were born when sailors caught sight of sirenians such as this manatee. Four species of sirenians—and no mermaids—exist today.

Sirenians: Dugongs and Manatees

Everyone knows what a mermaid looks like. She is half woman, half fish, and irresistibly beautiful. In some old stories she lures sailors to their deaths at sea. She is also imaginary, a creature of myth and legend.

Mermaids were called sirens in ancient Greek mythology. The mammal order Sirenia, which contains the sea cows, was named for these bewitching beings. Some people think that the idea of mermaids got started when sailors glimpsed sea cows on the ocean's surface, even though sirenians look nothing at all like most people's image of mermaids!

Sirenians are the only sea mammals that are herbivores. They are not purely vegetarian, however. Crabs and snails have been found in sirenian stomachs. Such prey lives in the sea grasses on which sirenians feed and is probably eaten along with the plants. But some manatees have also been seen eating dead fish and fish trapped in fishing nets

DUGONGS

Two kinds of sirenians exist today, dugongs and manatees. Dugongs are represented by a single surviving species, *Dugong dugon.* The dugong is a coastal animal that lives in shallow offshore waters. Its range includes the Red Sea, the Indian Ocean, Southeast Asia, northern Australia, the coast of China, and as far north as the southernmost islands of Japan. In the past it was seen around some island groups in the eastern Pacific, but it has since disappeared from much of that range. Some old writings suggest that the dugong once lived in the Mediterranean Sea as well, but if so, it has not been seen there for centuries.

Adult dugongs are typically 8 to 10 feet long (2.5 to 3 m) and weigh between 550 and 925 pounds (250 and 420 kg). Their thick gray-brown skin

The species *Dugong dugon* is the last living representative of a once-large family of sea mammals now known only from fossils. Extinct dugongs lived in many parts of the world, including the American coasts, where no dugongs have lived in modern times.

Spreading its strong, flexible upper lip, a dugong grazes on sea grass near the Pacific Ocean island nation of Vanuatu.

is sprinkled with sparse hairs and is often marked by scars, patches of algae, and barnacles, which are tiny, shelled marine creatures that also attach themselves to whales. Dugongs swim by moving their flukes, or tails, up and down, using their short, paddle-like flippers to change direction. They also "walk" on their flippers across the sea bottom as they graze.

Dugongs' mouths are well adapted for feeding on sea grasses. The mouth has a long, muscular upper lip in the shape of an upside-down U, with short, stiff bristles on each side. The lower lip is shorter and covered with pads of tough tissue. To eat, the dugong catches hold of grasses with its lower lip, wraps its flexible upper lip around the stems, pulls the grasses up by the roots, and stuffs them into its mouth. Dugongs usually feed in waters less than 16 feet (5 m) deep. Some researchers think that the animals rest in deeper waters farther from shore, moving into shallower zones to eat. They come to the surface to breathe every 1 to 3 minutes. Dugongs are marine animals that rarely enter fresh water.

This Dugong Is Long Gone

Sirenians today live only in warm tropical or subtropical waters, but it wasn't always that way. In 1741 a Russian exploring expedition spent a miserable, snowbound winter on the Commander Islands in the Bering Sea. The expedition's scientist, Georg Wilhelm Steller, found a species of huge dugong living in the cold waters around the islands. It became known as Steller's sea cow (also called the northern sea cow), *Hydrodamalis gigas*.

Scientists now know that *H. gigas* or its close relatives once lived along the rim of the North Pacific from Mexcio to Japan. By the time Europeans discovered the animal, though, it survived only near the Bering Sea islands. Some researchers think that hunting by prehistoric Pacific Rim peoples may have killed off this 24.5-foot-long (7.5-meter-long) dugong in most of its former range. Europeans finished the job. After reading Steller's description of the sea cow's thick, nutritious fat, Russian hunters swarmed to the Pacific in search of the slow-moving beasts. They were so successful that Steller's sea cow became extinct in 1768, twenty-seven years after Steller's discovery.

MANATEES

Manatees live in both fresh and salt water. There are three species. The West African manatee is about the size of a dugong. Its typical habitat is a shallow river mouth or a coastal lagoon or swamp, although the manatees can also be found some distance up certain rivers in Senegal and other West African nations. This species of manatee grazes on aquatic plants and also eats vegetation that hangs over the water.

The Amazonian species is the smallest manatee. Its maximum length is 9 feet (2.8 m), although many individuals are smaller. This species lives only in fresh water. It is found in South America's Amazon basin, where its typical habitat is large lakes or backwaters—areas of still water that are linked to rivers. The Amazonian manatee's range extends to the mouth of the Amazon River on the Atlantic coast, but this species does not leave the fresh water of the river.

The West Indian manatee is the biggest species. Average adults are slightly longer than dugongs and generally weigh more, because manatees have plumper bodies. Together the two subspecies of West Indian manatees (the Florida manatee and Antillean manatee) cover a range that extends from the southeastern United States to the coast of Brazil. West Indian manatees occupy a wider range of habitats than the other two

In Florida's Crystal River, a wintering territory for many Florida manatees, a youngster nurses from the mammary gland beneath its mother's flipper.

species. They are found in shallow offshore waters, bays, river mouths, and freshwater rivers and springs. During cold weather they often gather in large numbers near natural warm springs or places where power plants empty warm water into rivers.

In coastal waters West Indian manatees feed on sea grasses growing from the bottom, but in swamps and rivers they often eat floating vegetation. People have introduced West Indian manatees to the Panama Canal and to waterways in the South American nation of Guyana in order to control water hyacinth, a fast-growing floating plant that can choke rivers and canals. Florida also has serious problems with water hyacinth and other

The tail flukes of a mother and her calf show the damage that boat propellers do to Florida manatees. The adult manatee's tail (right) has been cut numerous times. The calf's is uninjured, for now.

A snorkeler in the Crystal River has an unforgettable encounter. Swimmers are urged not to harass the manatees or to approach them closely, but the manatees may approach the swimmers. The manatees never attack, but sometimes they seem gently curious.

plants that clog its river channels and boat marinas. Some Floridians believe that manatees could help solve that problem—if given the chance. Sadly, manatees live in peril in Florida and in most other parts of their range. Modern life has brought a threat for which manatees have no defense—power boats. Most manatees' backs are crisscrossed with scars from boat propellers. In some manatee habitats, local authorities have placed speed limits on boats, hoping to give manatees a chance to avoid propellers and to minimize injuries. Still, boats continue to take a deadly toll of the slow-moving mammals.

The walrus's ivory tusks have long made this marine mammal of the northern seas a hunter's prize. Walruses have also been a major food source for native peoples of the far north. Like seals, sea lions, sea otters, and polar bears, walruses are members of the carnivore order of mammals.

Seals, Walruses, Sea Otters, and Polar Bears

A polar bear crouches by a hole in the ice. On a chilly, snowy morning in the Arctic spring, everything is pale—the sky, the ice, and the great white bear. The whiteness of the scene is broken only by the bear's eyes and its black nose, and the circle of dark water whose edges lap at the ice. The polar bear is motionless for a long time. Suddenly, lightning-fast, it plunges its head and clawed forelegs into the hole. A moment later the bear backs away from the hole, dragging a ringed seal in its jaws. The seal's gray-spotted coat is smeared with blood. One carnivorous sea mammal has just preyed on another.

Most carnivores live on land, but three families in the order Carnivora are made up entirely of sea mammals—several different kinds of seals, the sea lions, and the walrus. Scientists group the families that contain these animals into a suborder called the pinnipeds (although some experts think that pinnipeds should be taken out of the order Carnivora and given their own order). Sea otters and polar bears are also considered marine mammals, but they belong to other carnivore families. They are the only members of those families that have adopted a marine way of life.

PINNIPEDS: SEALS, SEA LIONS, AND WALRUSES

There are three families of pinnipeds: the earless seals, which are also called true seals or hair seals; the eared seals and sea lions; and the walrus. The name *pinniped* is Latin for "feather-footed" or "wing-footed," but pinnipeds have no feathers or their feet—or anywhere else. The name refers to these animals' flat, paddle-like feet, which are shaped something like wings. The feet serve as flippers for swimming, but pinnipeds also use their flippers to pull themselves around on land.

Unlike cetaceans and sirenians, which never leave the water, pinnipeds are not fully aquatic animals. They depend on the land to breed, because they must leave the water to mate and give birth. For these activities, and sometimes also to rest, pinnipeds haul out (come ashore) onto beaches, ice, and rocks. The fact that pinnipeds have flippers instead of feet, however, is a sign that they have evolved to spend much more time in the water than on land. Few pinnipeds spend more than about forty-five days a year out of the water.

Pinnipeds eat a wide variety of marine life: krill (small

A female fur seal and her pup. Seals give birth on land, then introduce their pups to the sea within a few weeks of birth. A fur seal pup may spend more than a year with its mother before striking out for life on its own.

shrimplike animals), mollusks (shellfish), crabs, and fish. If a seal cannot swallow a fish whole, it seizes the fish in its jaws and shakes it until it breaks apart. Some people see pinnipeds as pests that destroy fish. In the Pacific Northwest, for example, salmon are a prized but declining fish resource. Salmon fishermen in the region argue that sea lions kill too many salmon, and debate rages about whether the sea lions themselves should be killed.

The full range of some pinniped species in the open ocean is not yet known. Most information about them comes from studies at or near their breeding sites. Located along coasts or on islands, these breeding sites may represent just a fraction of the animals' range. For example, the northern fur seal, *Callorhinus ursinus,* may be seen anywhere across the North Pacific Ocean but now breeds only on a handful of small islands, most of them in the Bering Sea.

Earless Seals

The family Phocidae has about nineteen species, including elephant, monk, hooded, beared, crabeater, leopard, ribbon, harp, ringed, and Weddell seals. Many of these phocids, as taxonomists call them, live in the cold waters around the north and south polar regions. But there are phocids in many other parts of the world, too.

The gray seal is native to the Atlantic coasts of Europe and northern North America. The northern elephant seal is found in the Pacific from southern Alaska to Mexico. The common or harbor seal is one of the most widespread species, with a range that includes the coasts of North America, Europe, and northeastern Asia.

Other species have much more limited ranges. The Caspian seal is found only in the Caspian Sea, a salty inland sea in central Asia. The Baikal seal is limited to Lake Baikal, a large body of fresh water in Siberia. The Hawaiian monk seal lives around a string of small islands in northwestern Hawaii.

Phocids are called earless seals because their sleek, streamlined heads have no visible ear flaps, or pinnae. Although these seals hear very

The gray seal is a phocid, a member of a widespread family of seals. These sleek-headed marine mammals are sometimes called the earless seals, because they lack visible ear flaps.

well both underwater and on land, they have small ear canals that are concealed by their coats of stiff hair. When they swim, phocids drive themselves forward with powerful strokes of their hind limbs, a pair of rear-pointing flippers at the back of their tapering bodies. On land, the hind limbs are useless, and phocids move by humping their bodies and wriggling forward, sometimes pulling with their front flippers while the rear flippers trail behind.

The smallest phocids are the Baikal seals, with a maximum length of 4.6 feet (1.4 m) and weight of just under 200 pounds (90 kg). The largest are the elephant seals, which can be up to 21 feet (6.5 m) long and weigh as much as 8,100 pounds (3,700 kg), which is more than 4 tons. These are not only the largest phocids but the largest pinnipeds. Female elephant seals are about half as long as males and considerably less massive.

Male elephant seals have large pouches of skin on their noses. Hanging over the seals' mouths, these look something like the trunks of elephants, although they are much shorter. The seal can inflate his proboscis, or nose, to make an ear-splittingly loud roar that sounds like the trumpeting of an elephant. During breeding season, the roars scare off or challenge rival males and warn intruders away from a male's territory. Among the hooded seals—a species found in the Arctic—males have a similar, but smaller, inflatable proboscis.

Eared Seals and Sea Lions

The fourteen or so otariids, members of the family Otariidae, are sometimes called eared seals because of their pinnae. These small ear flaps lie flat against the skin but are usually visible. All of the seals in this family are

A pair of male elephant seals roar at each other. Stand-offs such as this usually involve conflicts over territory. Occasionally they go beyond bellowing to wrestling or fightings, but most challenges are limited to a lot of noise.

Currents keep the waters around the Galapagos Islands in the Pacific Ocean cold and full of fish—an ideal habitat for the Galapagos sea lion.

known as fur seals because their coats are thicker and plushier than those of the earless seals. Eared seals have downy underfur for warmth topped by stiff guard hairs that protect it from water.

Eared seals or fur seals are found mostly in cooler waters in both the northern and southern hemispheres, although a few species inhabit sub-tropical regions, such as the west coast of Mexico. The otariids swim mostly with movements of the front parts of their bodies, using their front flippers to propel themselves through the water. On land, however, their rear flippers are much more useful than those of the phocids. Otariids can rotate their rear flippers forward and place them under the body, which allows these pinnipeds to walk or run on all fours. Although otariids do not cover long distances this way, over short distances they can move fast enough to outrun any human.

Half a dozen or so members of the otariid family are called sea lions because, like male lions on land, the male sea lions have manes or collars

INTERNAL ANATOMY OF A SEA LION

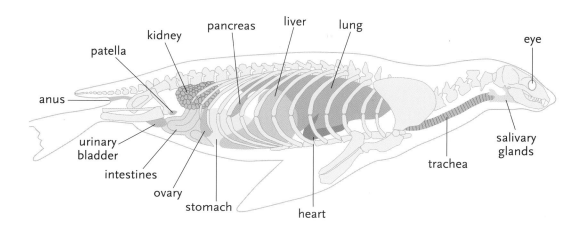

of long, dense fur. (Some male fur seals also have manes, but they are less noticeable than those of the sea lions). The mane may have evolved to protect the animals' necks and throats during fights over females, to impress the females, or both.

Although male sea lions are typically quite a bit larger than females, both sexes tend to be larger and stockier than fur seals. The largest species are the New Zealand sea lion, which inhabits the coastal waters of southern New Zealand and nearby small islands, and the northern or Steller's sea lion, which lives around the North Pacific from Japan to central California. The largest males of these species reach lengths of 11.5 feet (3.5 m) and weights of 500 pounds (227 kg).

Walrus

The family Odobenidae probably evolved in the North Pacific. At one time many species of walruses lived in that region. By about 2 million years ago, though, all but one of them had become extinct. The only surviving member of the family is *Odobenus rosmarus,* the walrus, which lives in the

These walruses have hauled out onto a rocky shore to breed, bask, or both.

coastal waters of the Arctic Ocean and neighboring seas, such as the Greenland Sea and the Bering Sea. Populations in different parts of this large range have evolved far enough apart that taxonomists consider the Pacific and Atlantic walruses to be separate subspecies.

Walruses range in size from 7 feet (just over 2 m) and 880 pounds (400 kg) for the smallest females to 11.5 feet (3.5 m) and 3,750 pounds (1,700 kg) for the largest males. They have short, coarse, sparse hair that they shed in summer and thick, stiff bristles around their mouths. Their most distinctive feature is their tusks. The upper canine teeth of both males and females keep growing throughout the animals' lives, reaching lengths of up to about 3 feet (almost 1 m) in males. Walruses have been observed using their curved tusks for anchoring themselves to ice while they sleep in the water, for pulling themselves out of the water, and for fighting with each other. Unfortunately for the walruses, people have also found uses for the animals' ivory tusks, which are prized as material for ornaments and jewelry. This is one reason walruses, like elephants, have been hunted heavily.

Walruses can turn their hind flippers forward, under the body, and use them together with the front flippers for moving around on land, although they are slower and less agile on land than eared seals and sea lions. When walruses come onto land, they favor isolated beaches and islands. A preferred habitat is pack ice in coastal waters. The animals haul out to rest or bask on the ice or on land in groups of several thousand, with much noisy skirmishing for position and fighting over territory. They mate in the water, but the females bear their young on the ice, or on land. Rough pads on the undersides of all four feet give walruses traction on ice.

Walruses feed on benthic prey—animals that live on the sea bottom—at depths of between 33 and 164 feet (10 and 50 m). The deepest recorded dive by a walrus was 262 feet (80 m). To feed, a walrus swims along with its vibrissae—the whiskers or bristles on its snout— brushing the bottom. When the vibrissae encounter something to eat, they maneuver the food toward the mouth. If the food is enclosed in a shell, the walrus clamps its lips on the shell and sucks out the meat. A walrus may eat thousands of clams in one feeding session. Clams and mussels are the main food items, but walruses occasionally catch fish and even prey on seals.

SEA OTTERS AND POLAR BEARS

Otters

These carnivores are aquatic relatives of weasels and ferrets. There are a dozen or so species of otters in the world, but most of them spend all or most of their time in fresh water. They are called river otters. Although a few species of river otters sometimes enter marine habitats such as the bays or coastlines near river mouths, they never go far from fresh water or from the shore. Only two species of otters are adapted to a true marine way of life in the sea. Even these otters remain close to shore and go on land from time to time.

The marine otter, *Lontra felina,* is one of the least-known otter species. It lives along the coast of western South America, especially in

A female marine otter navigates the coastal waters of Peru's Paracas National Park. Like their close relatives the sea otters, marine otters are an endangered species, at risk from illegal hunting, habitat loss, and pollution.

rocky areas. These otters feed by scrambling and diving among the rocks for worms, crustaceans, shellfish, and fish. Their hind feet have webbed toes and serve as flippers; their front feet are barely webbed. Some marine otters spend their entire lives in the sea, but others occasionally enter rivers.

Much more is known about the sea otter, *Enhydra lutris*. This playful and appealing marine mammal has been the subject of many television documentaries, and it is a popular attraction at zoos and marine parks. With an average length for males of about 5 feet (1.5 m) and a weight of just under 100 pounds (45 kg), sea otters are among the smallest sea mammals. Their range extends along the North Pacific coast from northern Japan to North America.

Sea otters sometimes haul out onto rocky islets and shores, but they spend most of their time at sea. In order to rest, otters raft, or float on their backs together. A favored habitat is forests of kelp, which is a giant seaweed that grows from the ocean bottom to the surface in offshore waters. Sea otters sleep on their backs on the surface of the water, and they may drape a few fronds of kelp over themselves to keep from drifting away in their sleep. By day they hunt among the towering kelp plants. Otters catch and eat fish, but more often they feed by diving to the bottom to locate crabs and shellfish. They bring their prey to the surface, where they often lie on their backs, resting the food on their stomachs while they pull it apart with their front paws and eat it. When dealing with particularly stubborn clam shells, sea otters use tools. They fetch stones from the sea bottom or from the shore and bang the stones and the shellfish together until something gives. An otter may keep a useful stone through a number of dives by tucking it into a fold or pocket of skin under its front legs.

Unlike other sea mammals, sea otters do not have thick layers of fat to keep them warm in the water. Instead, the otter has a thick coat of long underfur that traps air and holds it against the animal's body, where it is warmed by body heat and protected from moisture by the longer guard hairs on top.

A pair of sea otters is relaxing on the ocean's surface. Sea otters often eat in this position, holding their prey—usually crabs or clams—on their bellies while they manipulate it with their nimble front paws.

Under the rippling northern lights, a polar bear prowls its hunting grounds at the boundary between ice and ocean.

Polar Bears

Polar bears also have thick, warm fur, but it is not as dense as the otter's. The bear does, however, carry a layer of fat that it rebuilds every spring and summer. The polar bear's chief food is seals, but bears also eat sea birds and land animals as large as reindeer. In addition, when they get the chance, polar bears scavenge the carcasses of stranded whales. On land they devour berries, just as brown and black bears do. The fat they put on during the feeding season keeps the bears alive through the winter, when food is scarce. Male polar bears reach a maximum weight of 1,750 pounds (800 kg), while females typically weigh about half as much.

In many ways polar bears are typical bears. This is not surprising, since they split off from the rest of the bear family no more than a million years ago, a fairly short time in terms of evolution. Like other bears, polar bears generally live solitary lives, except for females who have cubs. The bears gather in groups only when there is some large food resource, such as a whale carcass, to draw them together.

Yet in adapting to life on the sea ice of the far north, polar bears developed some features that set them apart from other bears—and not just their unique white coats. Polar bears also have longer necks than other bears. This feature is useful for swimming because these bears typically swim with their heads held high and out of the water. The polar bear's feet are large, giving it a powerful swimming stroke. The feet are well padded with thick hair, which helps protect the bear from cold and from slipping on the ice.

The polar bear may be the newest sea mammal, but it shows many adaptations to an environment that is not just aquatic but also Arctic. An animal that is well adapted to an environment, however, can find itself in trouble if the environment changes. Right now, the world's climate is changing in ways that are not yet fully understood, but many leading scientists agree that it is getting warmer. Each year there is less sea ice in the northern waters—the polar bear's habitat is melting away. The skills that make the polar bear a formidable hunter on the ice will be useless if the ice disappears. Can polar bears change their ways to fit the changing climate? Will they continue to have a place in the wild, or are they doomed to survive only in zoos and protected parks? The polar bears' future is uncertain, and that is the case for many other sea mammals, too.

A polar bear slips silently from an ice floe into the icy water. Polar bears around the Arctic have evolved to hunt on the region's pack ice. What will become of them if the ice continues to disappear?

Harp seal pups, called "whitecoats" for their snowy fur, have drawn the attention of many people who want to protect sea mammals or to end cruelty to animals. Each year Canadian sealers club, shoot, and skin several hundred thousand of these young animals, main to support the trade in fur coats.

An Uncertain Future

The baiji or Yangtze River dolphin used to be the world's rarest and most endangered cetacean. Its population shrank from about 400 individuals in 1980 to only 13 in 1997. But the baiji no longer holds the title of world's rarest cetacean. In 2007 researchers declared it extinct after a six-week expedition failed to find any trace of the baiji in its former range. Even if a few individuals survive here and there, unseen by the searchers, there are still too few to keep the species alive and healthy. The baiji is gone.

Before the baiji went extinct, the Japanese sea lion was wiped out in the late 1950s by hunters who wanted its meat (for food), its skin (for leather), its organs (for folk remedies thought to have medical value), and its whiskers (for pipe cleaners). The Steller's sea cow was driven into extinction nearly two centuries before that, and some whale species came close to being wiped out by nineteenth- and early-twentieth-century hunters. Today sea mammals face perils that may be even more serious.

In 2007 the baiji was declared extinct in the wild.

NEW THREATS

The sea otter's dense, soft fur does an excellent job of insulating the otter against cold water. It does such a good job that, beginning in the middle of the eighteenth century, Russians, Europeans, and Americans destroyed sea otter populations in many areas. The seals were hunted by the thousands for their fur.

Today, sea otters are legally protected as an endangered species in the United States and many other nations, and they are making a come-back in some parts of their former range. In California, the number of otters more than doubled between 1968 and 2006—from 1,300 to 3,000. The California sea otter is a marine mammal success story.

Fur hunters are no longer a grave threat to the otter's survival, although some hunting takes place. Poaching, or illegal hunting, takes an occasional toll on otters but is more harmful to other sea mammals. In addition, most countries that have laws protecting marine mammals also allow native peoples who traditionally lived by hunting marine mammals to kill a certain number of them each year. This is called subsistence hunting, or hunting to survive, and some traditional cultures regard it as both a tradition and a right. Environmentalists and animal-rights activists sometimes protest such hunts as unnecessary and damaging to endangered species, but subsistence hunting is not the biggest threat to sea otters and other marine mammals today.

Each year, fishing nets and lines trap and drown up to 300,000 whales and other sea mammals. The dead animals, killed by accident, are called bycatch in the fishing industry. But even the death toll from bycatch may not be the worst thing the animals face.

A dead dolphin lies washed up on the Black Sea coast of Bulgaria. According to local veterinary and environmental officials who later examined the body, the most likely cause of death was drowning after becoming entangled in fishing nets.

Oil spills from tanker ships are deadly to otters. The otter's fur is its only insulation. If the fur becomes dirty and the animal can't clean it, the fur no longer works as insulation, and the otter is likely to die of exposure or from trying to lick the oil from its body. Up to 5,000 sea otters were killed by a single spill in 1989, when the *Exxon Valdez* ran aground on rocks in the Gulf of Alaska. But in early 2007, when dead and sick sea otters and orphaned otter pups began washing ashore in California, there was no evidence of a spill.

Looking elsewhere for a clue, researchers suggested that otters were getting sick because their environment is sick. Pollutants such as pesticides, industrial waste, and sewage wash into the oceans. Such substances could have contaminated the beds of clams and the other food on which the otter depends.

Or perhaps the problem is something bigger and harder to fix, such as global warming. Even a slow, gradual rise in the world's temperature could be enough to disturb the delicate balance of life in the oceans, with unknown results. A biologist at the University of Washington, however, has found a way to let marine mammals join the battle against global warming. By placing small recording devices on the backs of

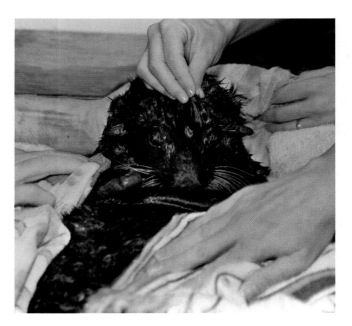

After the *Exxon Valdez* spill in 1989, volunteers raced to save the lives of endangered sea mammals such as this otter, being cleaned at a rescue center. Similar efforts are needed to clean imperiled sea mammals and birds whenever oil spills into the world's waters.

The Vanishing Vaquita

The world's most endangered marine mammal is a 5-foot (1.5-m) porpoise with the scientific name *Phoecena sinus.* It lives only in the northern part of the Gulf of California, the long arm of water between mainland Mexico and the Baja Peninsula, where it is called the vaquita or desert porpoise. It has a black stripe on each side of its head, a black circle around each eye, and curved black lips that seem to smile. Robert Pitman and Lorenzo Rojas-Bracho, scientists who have studied the vaquita, have called it "Mona Lisa with black lipstick."

In 2007 Pitman and Rojas-Bracho reported that fewer than 200 of these small porpoises remained. The biggest threat to their survival is hard-to-see gill nets that entangle and drown air-breathing sea mammals like porpoises. Although the Mexican government has established a vaquita refuge in the Gulf, fishermen continue to use gill nets inside the refuge. Unless conservationists can raise funds to work with the poor fishermen of the region, training them for better jobs or teaching them how to catch fish without killing porpoises, the vaquita will soon become extinct. As Pitman and Rojas-Bracho put it, human activity threatens to "wipe that little black smile off the face of the Earth forever."

The dark body of this vaquita lies in the center of a fisherman's catch.

In 2005 several pods of pilot whales beached themselves on the Australian island of Tasmania. Volunteers managed to save some of the stranded whales by returning them to the water, but more than a hundred died. Scientists do not yet know why whales and dolphins occasionally go off course and beach themselves, often with fatal results.

three narwhals, she was able to track their movements and develop a more accurate picture of water temperatures and currents around the North Pole. Scientists hope that narwhals will help them get reliable information about the loss of the Arctic ice pack and other changes brought by global warming.

There are signs that things are not going well for the world's sea mammals. Several mass strandings of beaked whales have taken place around the world since the beginning of the century. There have always been strandings, in which a whale or a group of whales beach themselves. Stranded whales cannot usually get back into the sea on their own. Without human help, they die. Many beach communities have organized volunteer groups to help stranded whales and dolphins, in the hope of saving them. Even mass strandings are not new—an Oregon beach was covered with stranded sperm whales in 1979. Some researchers, however, think that the strandings are becoming more frequent. Many fear that the problem is undersea noise pollution.

In addition to the ever-growing noise of ship traffic, the ocean basins now crackle and hum with man-made sounds, including long-range military sonar. The sound waves produced by sonar equipment are very similar to the "pings" of cetacean echolocation. There is some evidence that marine mammals can be confused, disoriented, or even hurt by this barrage of sound. The question of whether sonar is harmful to the animals ended up in court in 2007 when the Natural Resources Defense Council (NRDC) and other environmental groups sued the U.S. Navy to stop a "war games" military exercise that would have involved extremely loud sonar in California's offshore waters. A federal judge sided with the NRDC and declared that the Navy had to protect the marine life. However, a federal appeals court overturned the judge's decision, declaring that the Navy could use the high-powered sonar in as many as eleven training exercises, despite the threat to wildlife. The fight over high-powered, long-range sonar is far from over, however. The NRDC continues to seek a permanent ban on the use of this controversial technology.

SEA MAMMAL CONSERVATION

The World Conservation Union (IUCN) is an international association of conservation and wildlife agencies that monitors the status of animals and plants around the world. Its 2006 report listed more than forty species of marine mammals as critically endangered, endangered, vulnerable, or near threatened. Among them were the entire order Sirenia, the Steller's or northern sea lion, the Hawaiian and Mediterranean monk seals, the sea otter and marine otter, and twenty-five species of whales and dolphins.

Concern for marine mammals is not new. Since the late nineteenth century, governments and regulating agencies have been trying to control how marine mammals are used. The first agreements concerned the harvest of seals in Antarctica. Then, in 1948, the nations of the world established the International Whaling Commission (IWC) to govern the whaling industry. Since that time, large-scale commercial whaling has come to an end, although a few nations—mostly Japan and Norway—have resumed limited hunting of whales. Some of these hunts are said to be for "scientific" purposes, but whale meat ends up in food markets.

Within the United States and its waters, the treatment of sea mammals is governed by the Marine Mammal Protection Act (MMPA), which became law in 1972. The act made it illegal not just to hunt marine mammals in U.S. territory but also to import marine mammals or products made from them into the country. But although the MMPA clamps down on deliberate hunting, and the Endangered Species Act of 1973 is supposed to protect endangered marine mammals *and* their habitats, the future of marine mammals in America and the world is far from secure.

Vacationers in Hawaii occasionally encounter Hawaiian monk seals swimming in offshore waters or basking on beaches. The endangered seals are protected by law, and both lifeguards and local citizens will remind newcomers to keep their distance from the marine mammals.

Silhouetted against the sunset, a South African seal perches atop a rock at the ocean's edge. Seals are creatures of both land and sea, while some other marine mammals dwell only in the oceans. All sea mammals, however, are links between the mammals of the land—including humans—and the life of the oceans, where all life began.

Fortunately, sea mammals arouse strong passions in many people who see them—people who may fight, or vote, to protect whales, manatees, sea otters, and their habitat.

Marine mammals are what scientists call indicator species. Their well-being is a sign of the overall health of the ocean and its food chains. Conserving marine mammals may call for more than ending illegal hunting and netting. It may require nations to tackle such problems as chemical and noise pollution and global warming. To save the sea mammals, people may have to save the sea.

adapt—To change or develop in ways that aid survival in the environment.

anatomy—The physical structure of an organism.

ancestral—Having to do with lines of descent or earlier forms.

aquatic—Having to do with water; living in water (fresh or salt).

bycatch—Animals accidentally caught during fishing operations; often seals and dolphins.

carnivore—An animal that eats meat other animals, including fish and shellfish.

cetacean—Member of the Cetacea, the group of animals that includes whales, dolphins, and porpoises.

conservation—Action or movement aimed at protecting and preserving wildlife or its habitat.

convergent evolution—Process in which groups of animals evolved separately but have similar features because they are adapted to similar habitats or ways of life.

crustacean—Hard-shelled invertebrate (animal without a spine) that lives in the water, such as a shrimp, crab, or lobster.

echolocation—A method of sensing the underwater environment by bouncing sound waves off objects; sonar, a technological form of echolocation, is used on boats and submarines.

evolution—The pattern of change in life forms over time, as new species, or types of plants and animals, develop from old ones.

evolve—To change over time.

extinct—No longer existing; died out.

fluke—A broad, flattened tail.

genetic—Having to do with genes, material made of DNA inside the cells of living organisms. Genes carry information about inherited characteristics from parents to offspring and determine the form of each organism.

herbivore—An animal that eats plants.

mammal—Warm-blooded animal that gives birth to live young and nurses the young with milk from mammary glands.

marine—Having to do with the ocean.

migration—Seasonal movement, sometimes in large groups, between two territories or locations.

organism—Any living thing.

paleontology—The study of ancient life, mainly through fossils.

pinniped—Member of the Pinnipedia, a group of animals that includes seals, sea lions, and walruses.

zooplankton—Tiny drifting or floating animal life, including both small organisms and the eggs or larvae of larger organisms.

porpoise—Cetacean that is closely related to dolphins, but smaller, beakless, and with flat teeth instead of cone-shaped teeth like other cetaceans.

sirenian—A manatee or dugong (sirenians are sometimes called sea cows).

taxonomy—The scientific system for classifying living things, grouping them in categories according to similarities and differences, and naming them.

terrestrial—Living on the ground.

vertebrate—An animal with a backbone.

warm-blooded—Producing heat inside the body by digesting food for energy (in cold-blooded animals, body temperature is determined by the temperature of the outside world).

SEA MAMMAL

CLASS

ORDER   Cetaceans

SUBORDER   toothed whales   baleen whales

FAMILY

<u>10 families</u>

sperm whale
pygmy and dwarf
   sperm whales
beluga and narwhal
beaked whales
dolphins, pilot whales,
   and orcas
porpoises
river dolphins (4 families)

<u>4 families</u>

gray whale
pygmy right whale
bowhead and right whales
rorquals

SPECIES

FAMILY TREE

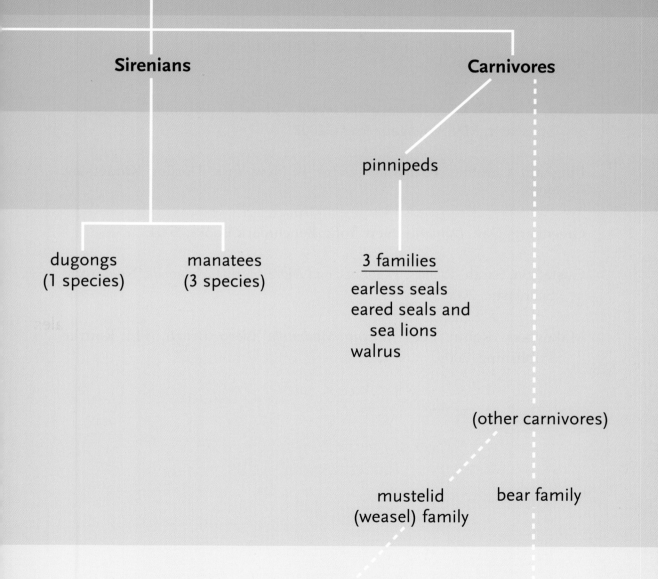

MAMMALS

Sirenians

Carnivores

pinnipeds

dugongs
(1 species)

manatees
(3 species)

<u>3 families</u>

earless seals
eared seals and
sea lions
walrus

(other carnivores)

mustelid
(weasel) family

bear family

sea otter
marine otter

polar bear

FURTHER READING

Baird, Robin W. *Killer Whales of the World: Natural History and Conservation.* Stillwater, MN: Voyageur Press, 2002.

Bingham, Caroline. *Whales and Dolphins.* New York: Dorling Kindersley, 2003.

Greenberg, Dan. *Dolphins.* New York: Benchmark Books, 2004.

Gustafson, Sarah. *Whales, Dolphins, and More Marine Mammals,* New York: Scholastic, 2005.

Makowski, Robin Lee. *Marine Mammals.* Vero Beach, FL: Rourke Publishing, 2005.

WEB SITES

http://nmml.afsc.noaa.gov/education/marinemammals.htm

This student-oriented site maintained by U.S. government science and wildlife agencies offers introductions to all types of sea mammals, with a guide to taxonomy.

http://www.tolweb.org/Cetacea/15977

The Cetaceans page of the Tree of Life Web Project, hosted by the University of Arizona, features evolutionary information on whales, dolphins, and porpoises.

http://animaldiversity.ummz.umich.edu/site/accounts/information/ Sirenia.html

The Animal Diversity Web of the University of Michigan Museum of Zoology offers this pags about manatees and dugongs, with emphasis on their evolutionary relationships.

http://www.otternet.com/index.htm

This kid-friendly site focuses on otters, with pictures, fun facts, and audio recordings of otter sounds.

http://www.gma.org/marinemammals/index.html

The Gulf of Maine Aquarium's Marine Mammals page focuses on whales but has information about other varieties of sea mammals.

http://www.aquaticmammals.org

Devoted to preserving marine mammal species, this kid-friendly site features many videos of sea mammals in their natural habitats, as well as information about threats to these species.

http://www.ammpa.org

The Alliance of Marine Mammal Parks and Aquariums operates this site to provide information about the care, study, and conservation of sea mammals.

http://www.animalbehaviorarchive.org/link.do?destination=marine

Part of Cornell University's Animal Behavior site, this page offers dozens of sound recordings of marine mammal communications, as well as some videos.

http://www.nwr.noaa.gov/Marine-Mammals

The National Marine Fisheries Service's Marine Mammals page has information about U.S. laws and regulations concerning whales, dolphins, seals, and other marine mammals.

http://www.iwcoffice.org/index.htm

The Web site of the International Whaling Commission IWC), which regulates the hunting and protection of whales for most countries, has information about the taxonomy, life histories, and conservation status of cetaceans.

The author found these sources especially helpful when researching this book.

Berta, Annalisa, et al. *Marine Mammals: Evolutionary Biology.* 2nd edition. Burlington, MA, and London: Academic Press, 2006.

Edgar, Blake. "Evolutionary Medicine and Swimming Sloths." *California Wild: The Magazine of the California Academy of Sciences.* Volume 48:4, Fall 1995, online at http://www.calacademy.org/calwild/1995fall/stories/horizons.html

Lovgren, Stefan. "China's Rare River Dolphin Now Extinct, Experts Declare." *National Geographic News,* December 14, 2006, online at http://news.nationalgeographic.com/news/2006/12/061214-dolphin-extinct.html

Nowak, Ronald M. *Marine Mammals of the World.* Baltimore and London: Johns Hopkins University Press, 2003.

Pitman, Robert L. and Lorenzo Rojas-Bracho. "How Now, Little Cow?" *Natural History.* July/August 2007, vol. 116, Number 6, pp. 28-32.

Reynolds, John E. III and Sentiel A. Rommel. *Biology of Marine Mammals.* Washington, DC: Smithsonian Institution Press, 1999.

Shirihai, Hadoram and Brett Jarrett. *Whales, Dolphins, and Other Marine Mammals of the World.* Princeton, NJ: Princeton University Press, 2006.

Twiss, John R., Jr. and Randall R. Reeves. *Conservation and Management of Marine Mammals.* Washington, D.C.: Smithsonian Institution Press, 1999.

Page numbers in **boldface** are illustrations.

A B O U T   T H E   A U T H O R

Rebecca Stefoff is the author of a number of books on scientific subjects for young readers. She has explored the world of plants and animals in Marshall Cavendish's Living Things series and in several volumes of the AnimalWays series, also published by Marshall Cavendish (the Family Trees series). She has authored several books in the Family Trees series. Stefoff has also written about evolution in *Charles Darwin and the Evolution Revolution* (Oxford University Press, 1996), and she appeared in the *A&E Biography* program on Darwin and his work. Stefoff lives in Portland, Oregon. You can learn more about her and her books at www.rebeccastefoff.com.